WinterScapes
COLORING BOOK

JESSICA MAZURKIEWICZ

DOVER PUBLICATIONS, INC.
MINEOLA, NEW YORK

The thirty-one designs in this coloring collection feature an assortment of winter motifs, from hot chocolate and marshmallows, snowflakes, and skis, to a variety of arctic wildlife such as penguins and reindeer. Part of Dover's *Creative Haven* series for the experienced colorist, each illustration takes up the entire page, and is enclosed in a decorative border for a finished look. Plus, the perforated pages make displaying your work easy.

Copyright
Copyright © 2014 by Dover Publications, Inc.
All rights reserved

Bibliographical Note
WinterScapes Coloring Book is a new work, first published by Dover Publications, Inc., in 2014.

International Standard Book Number
ISBN-13: 978-0-486-79186-9
ISBN-10: 0-486-79186-6

Manufactured in the United States by RR Donnelley
79186611   2015
www.doverpublications.com

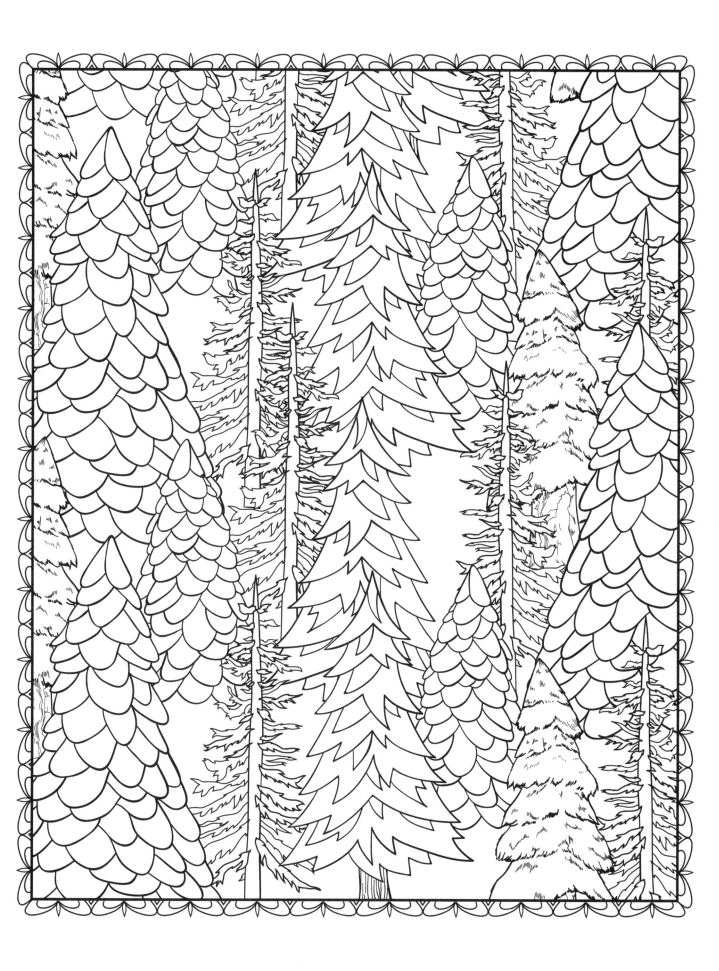

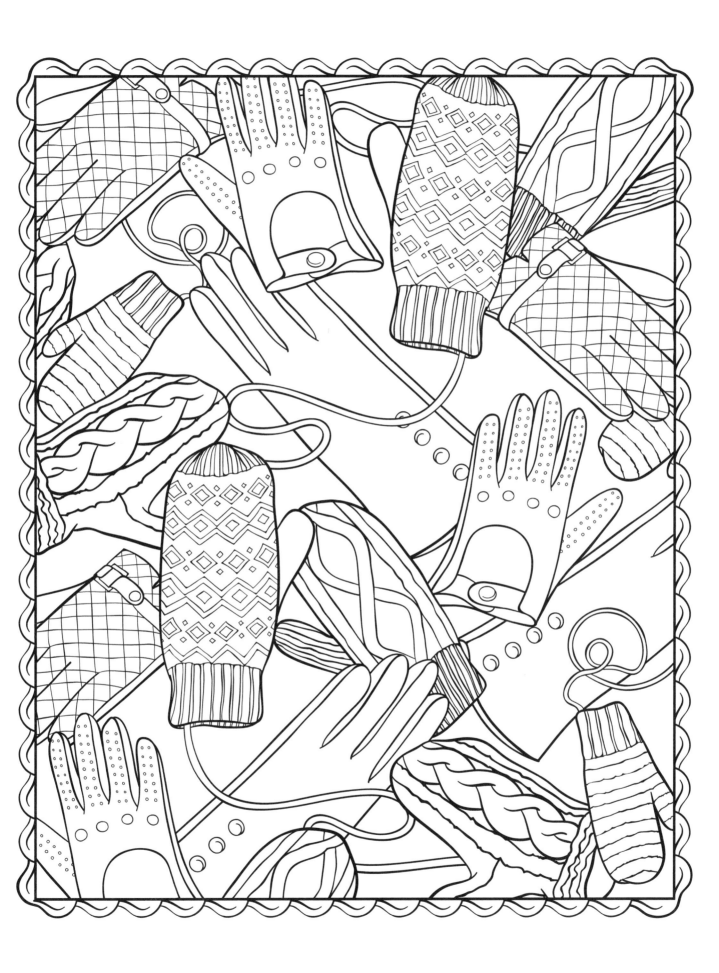

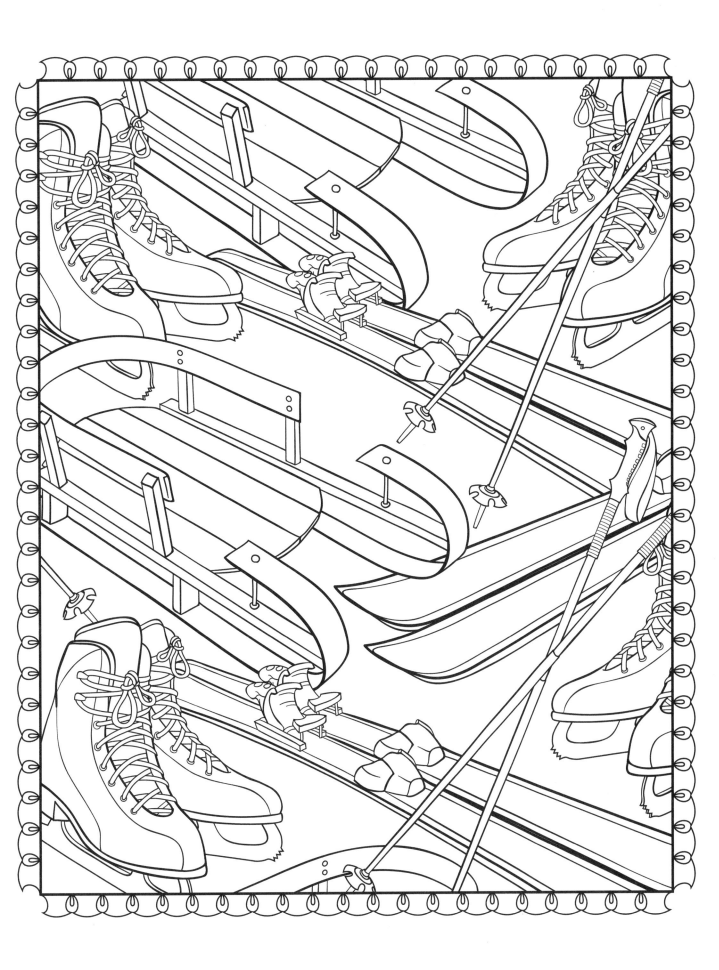